This Monster Truck Coloring Book Belongs to

____

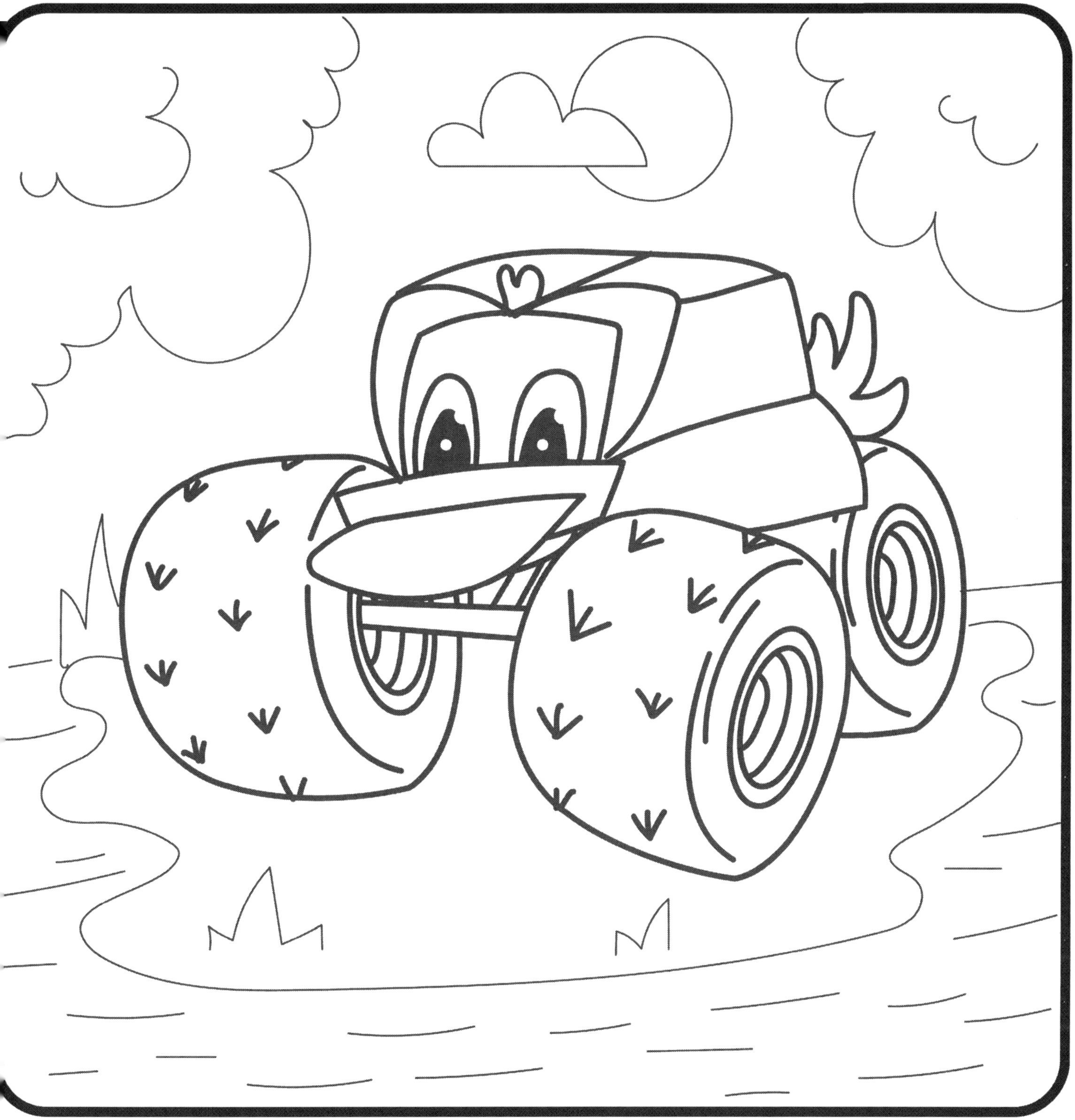

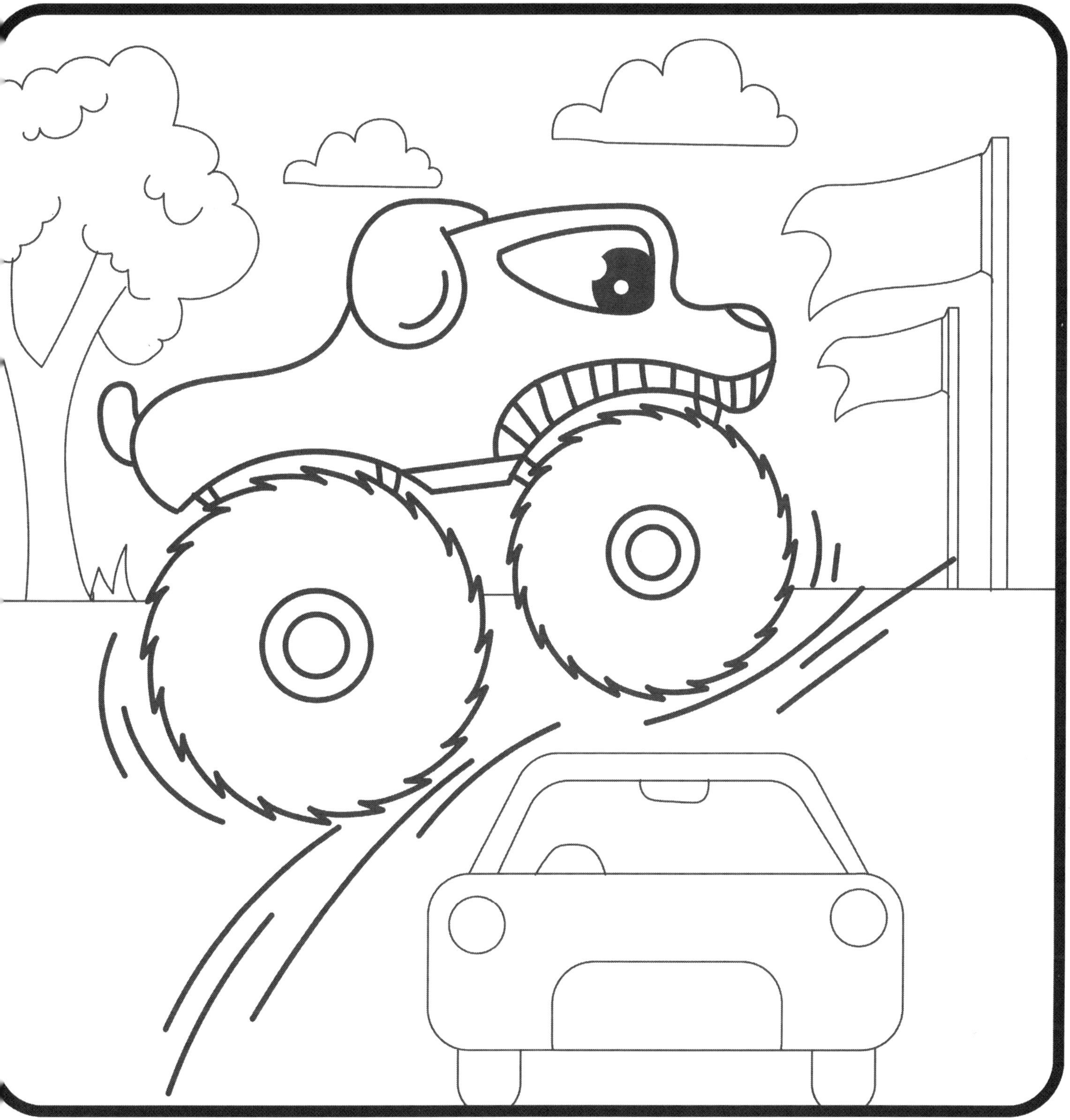

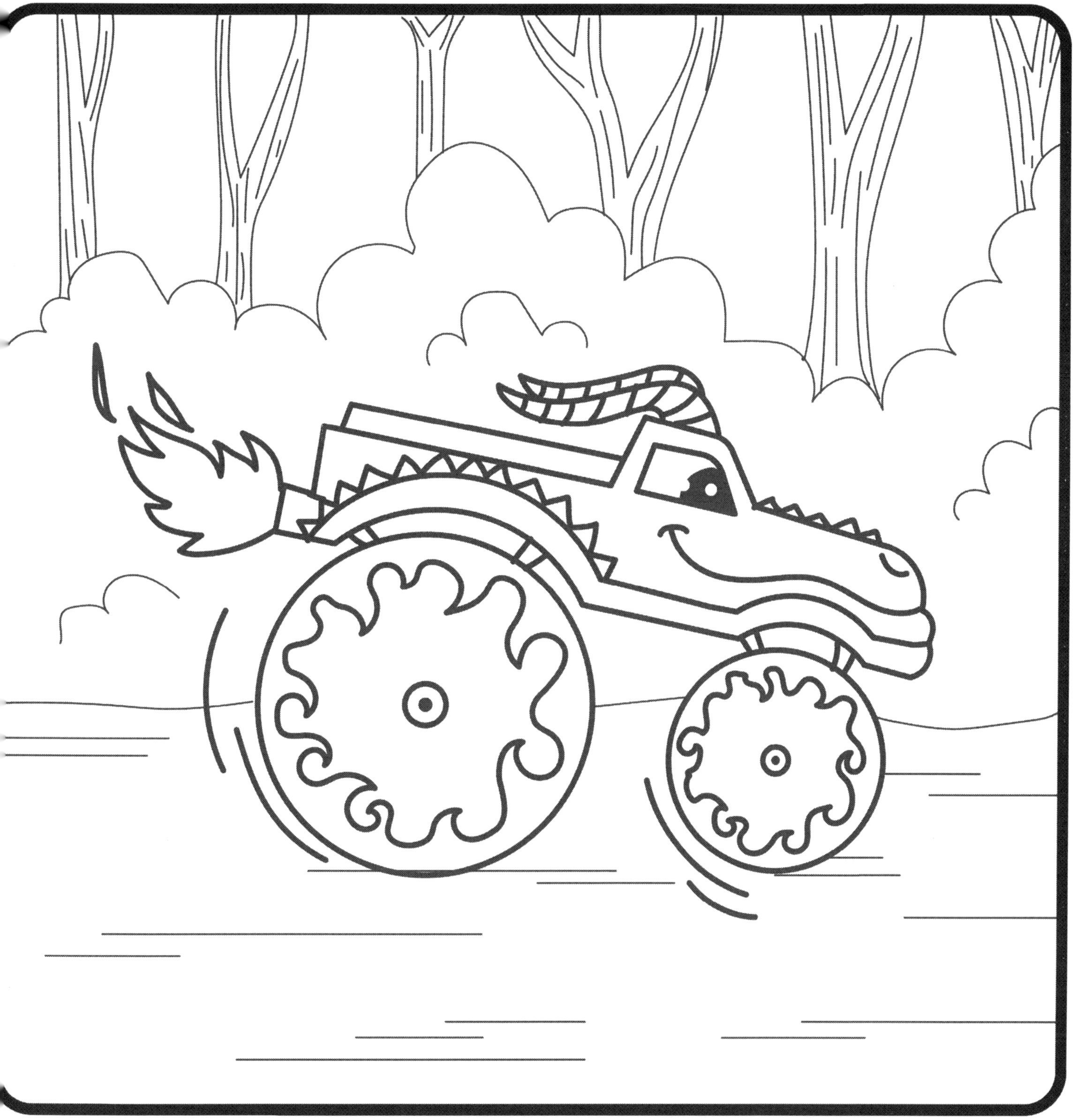

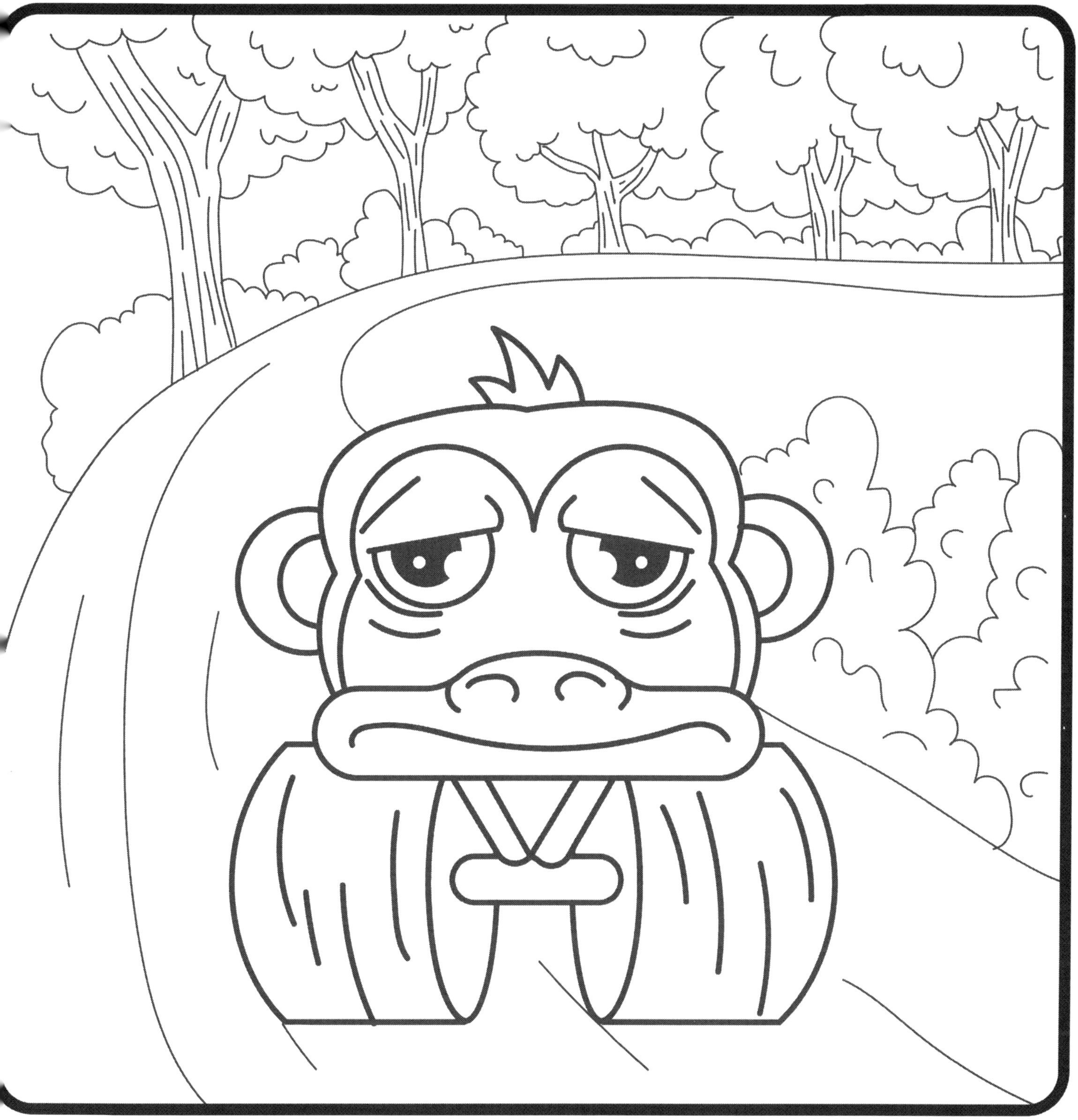

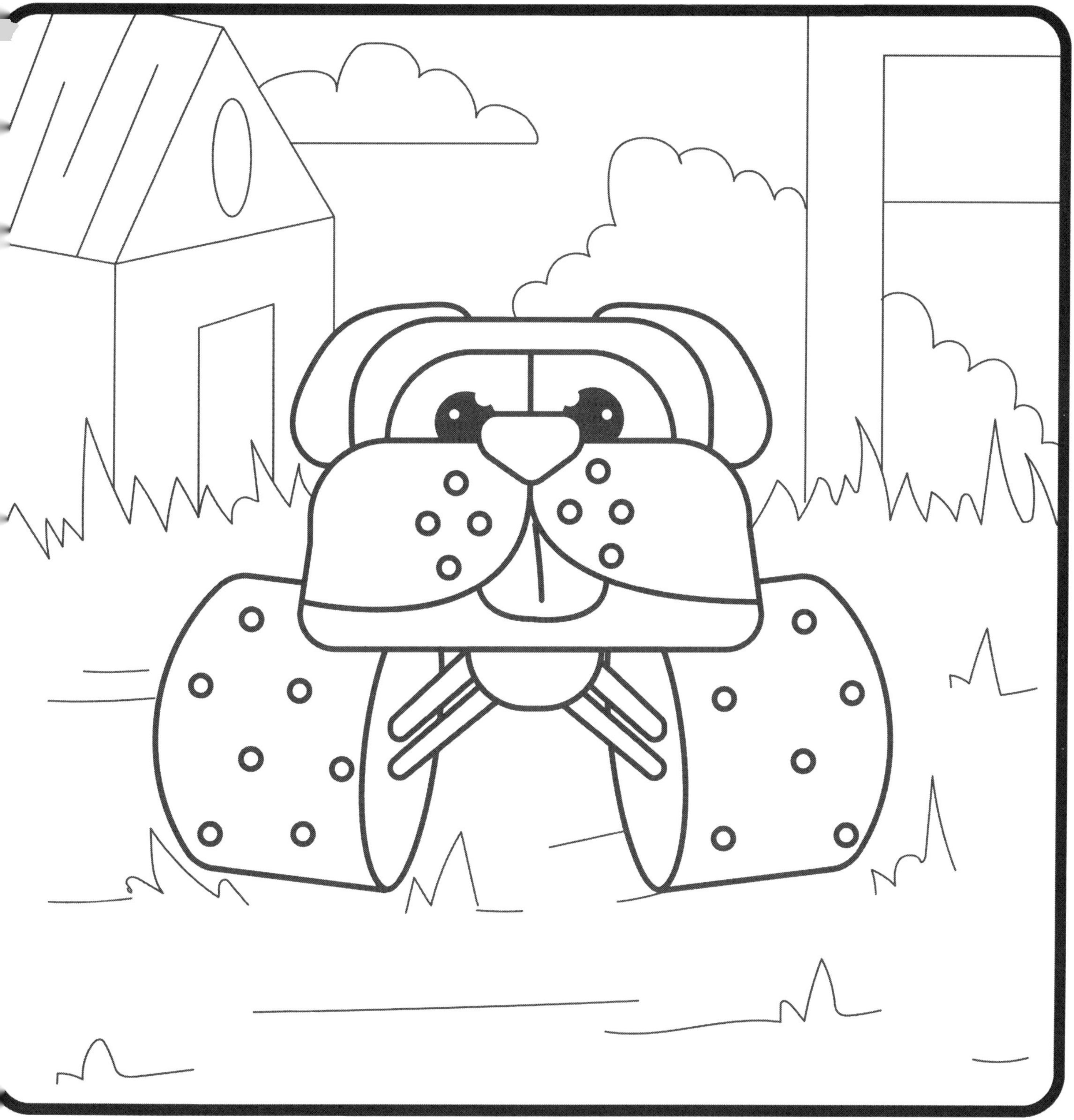

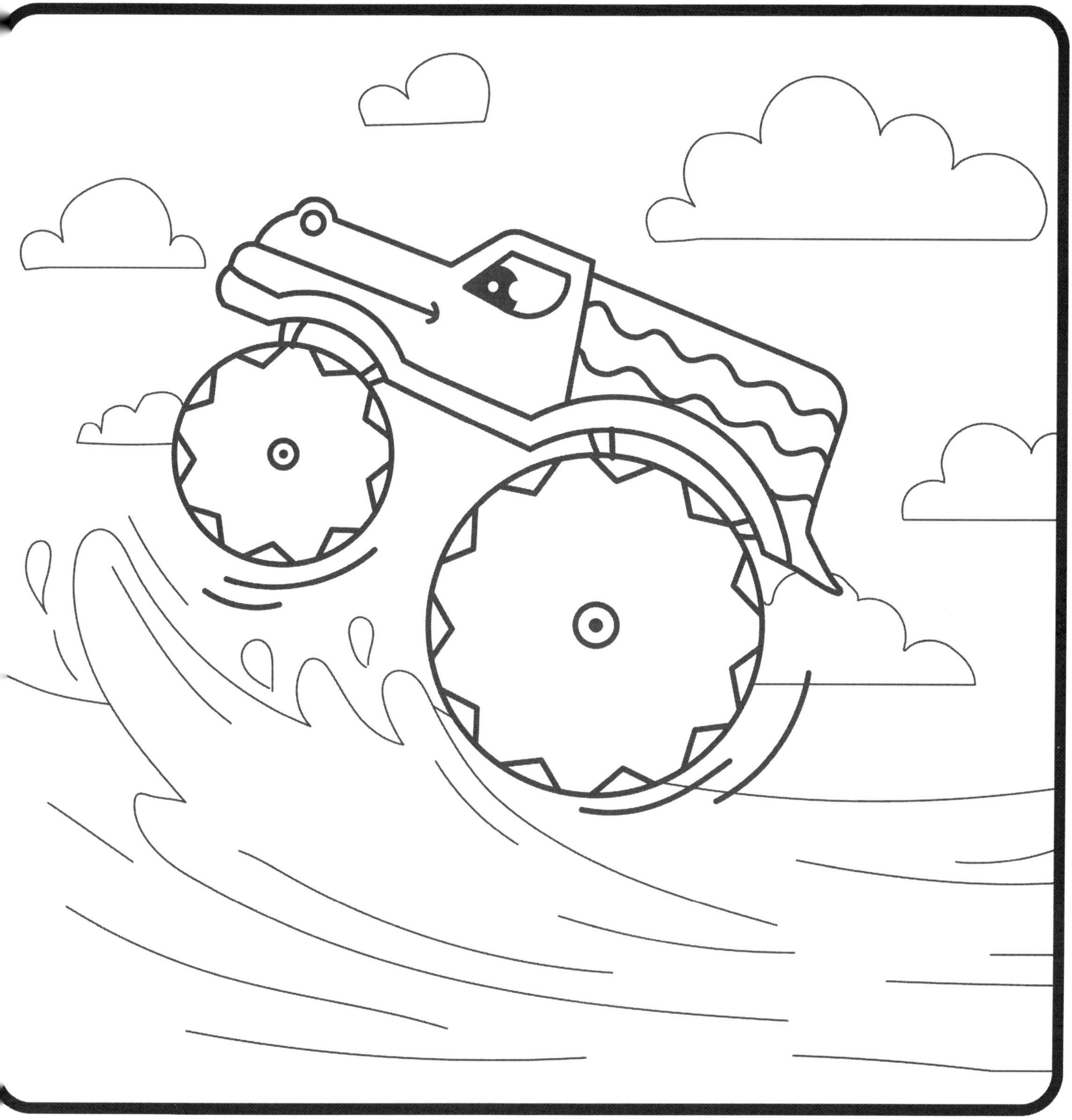

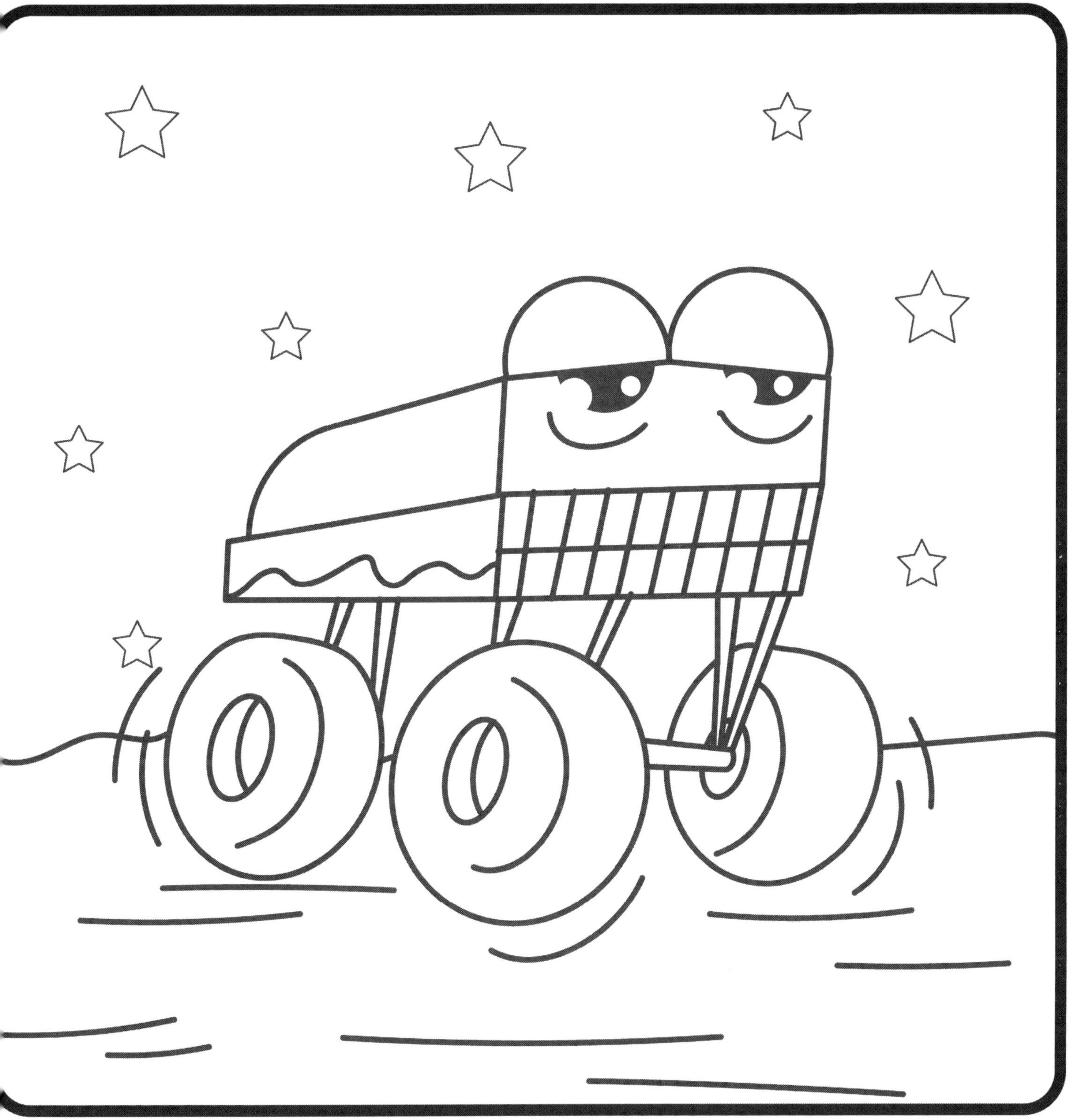

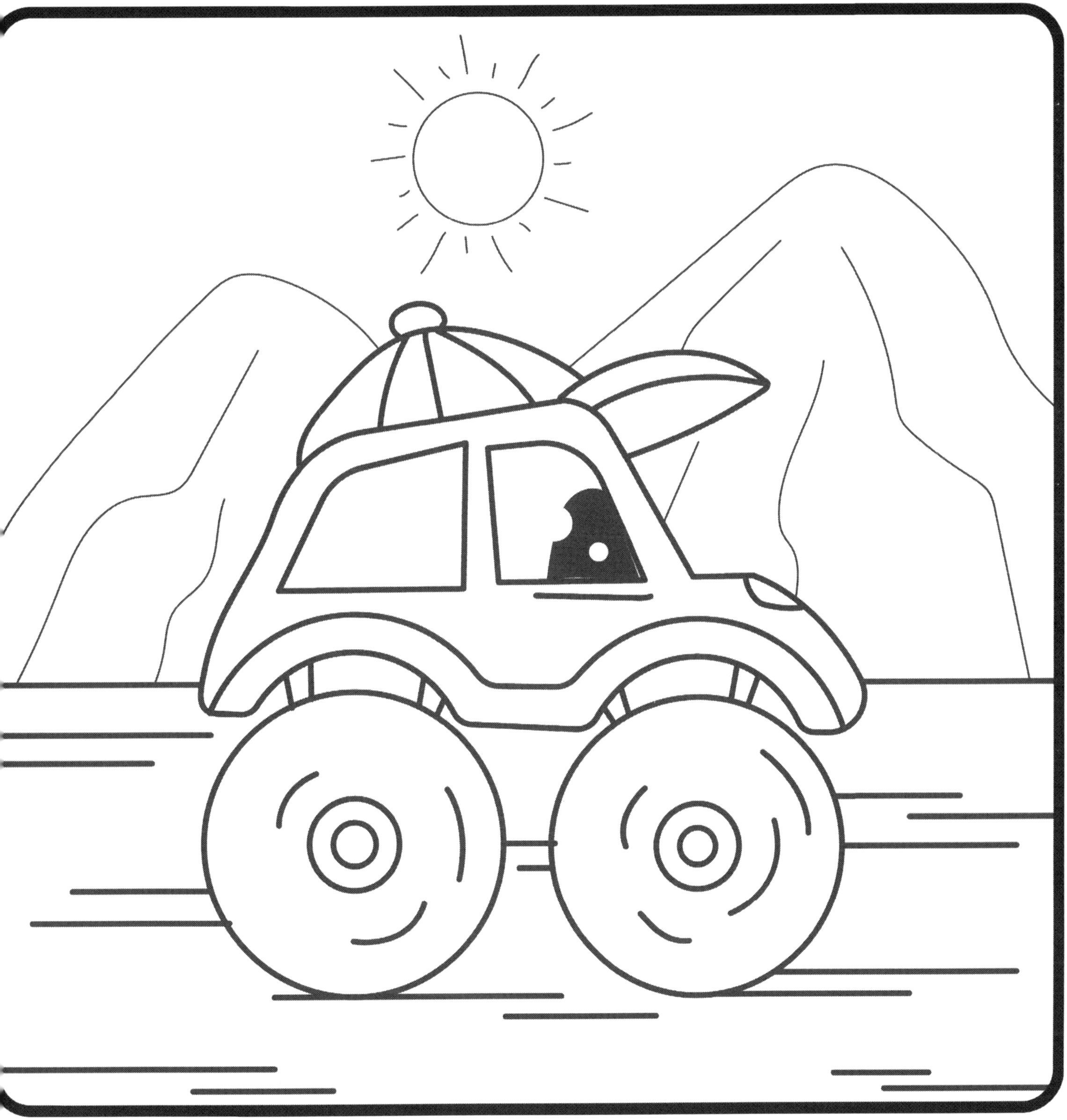

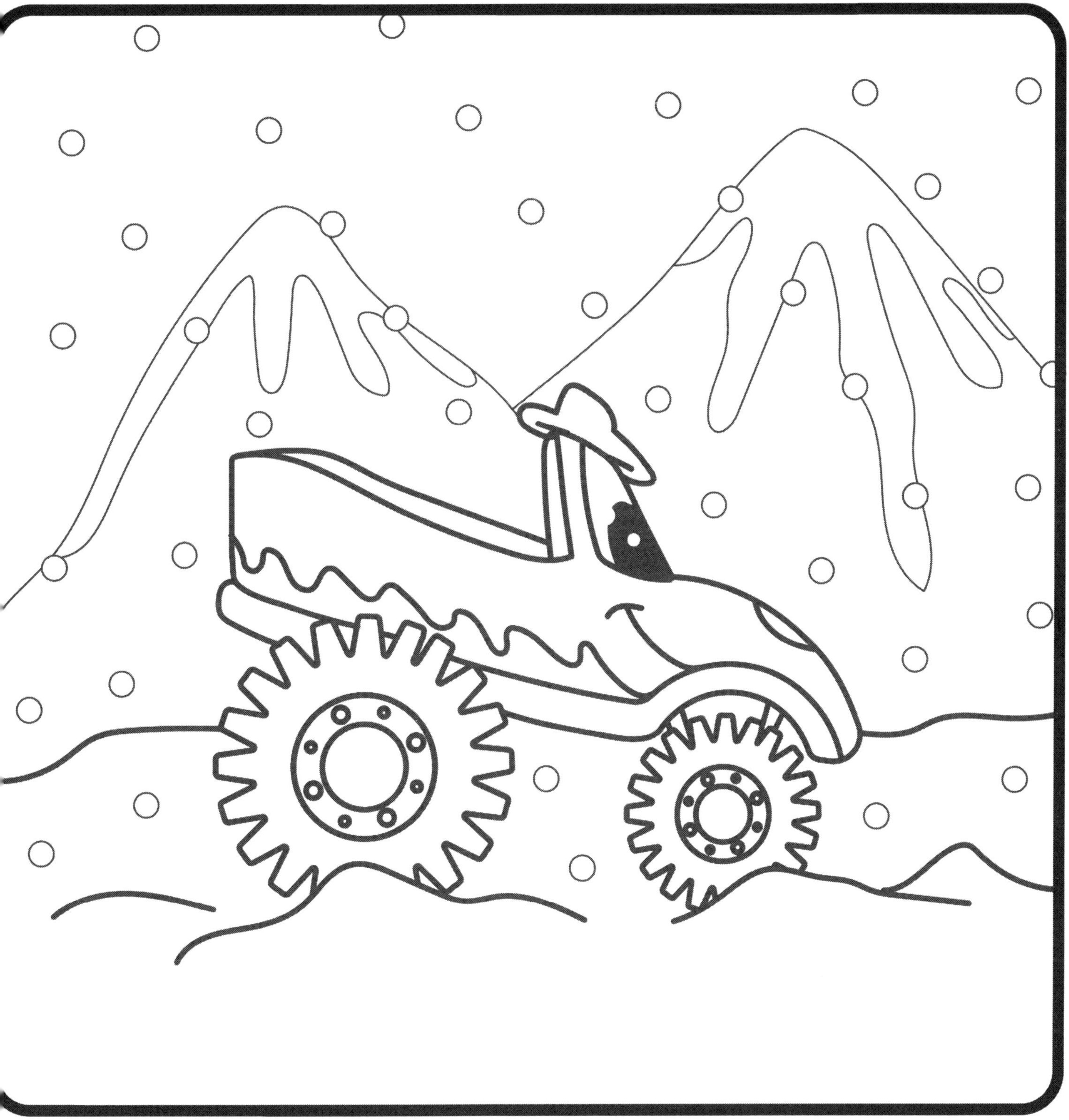

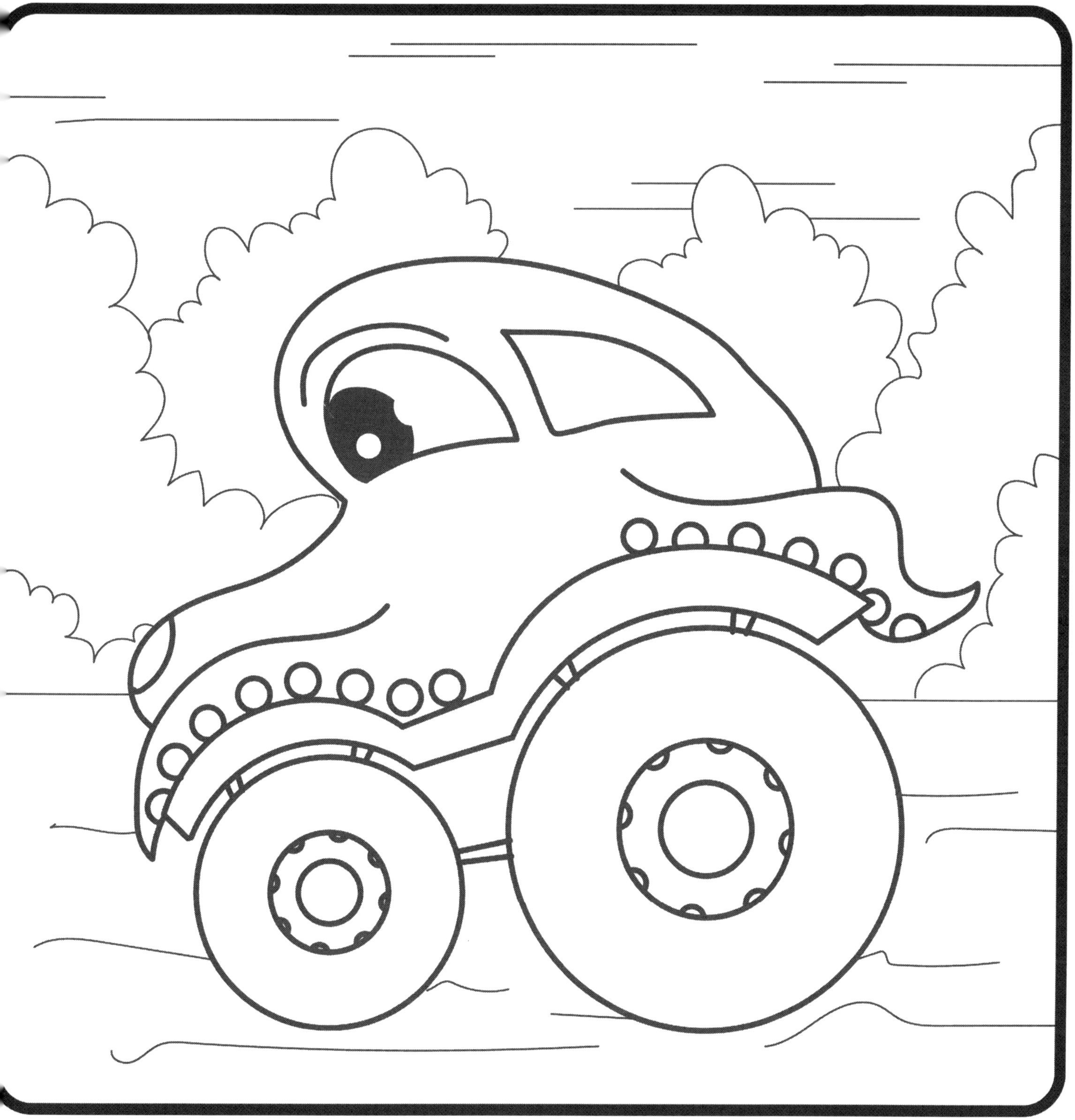

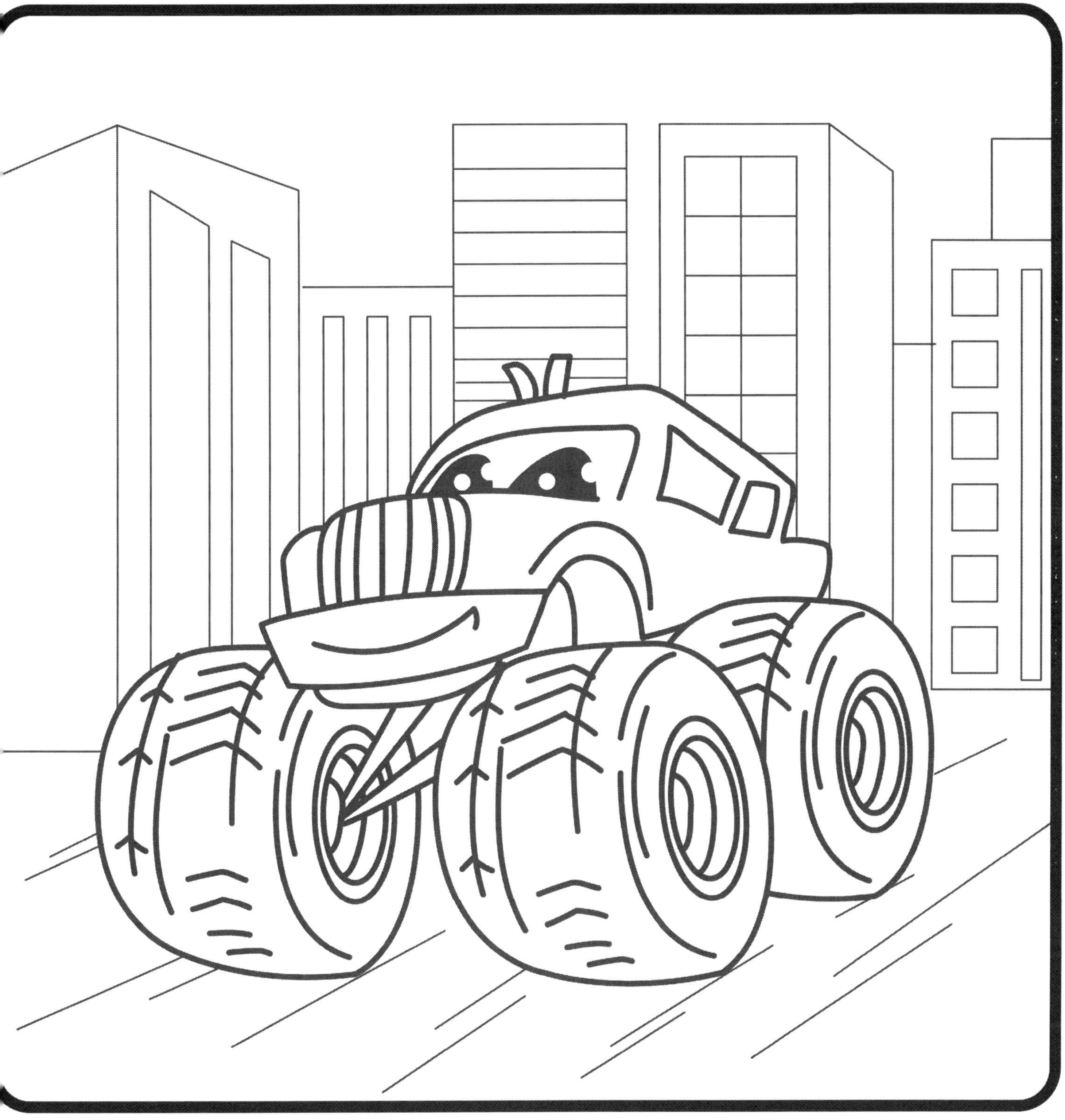

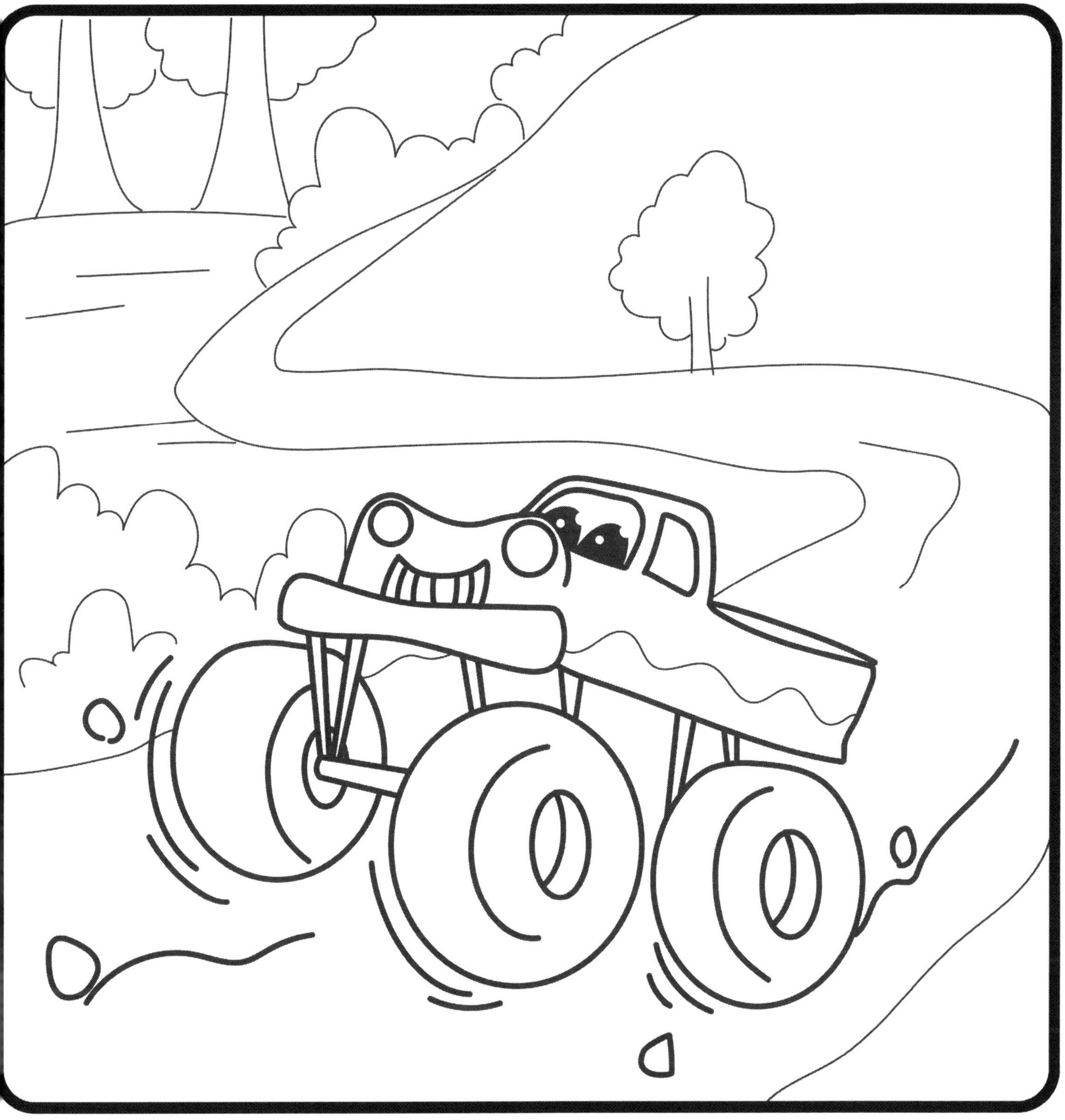

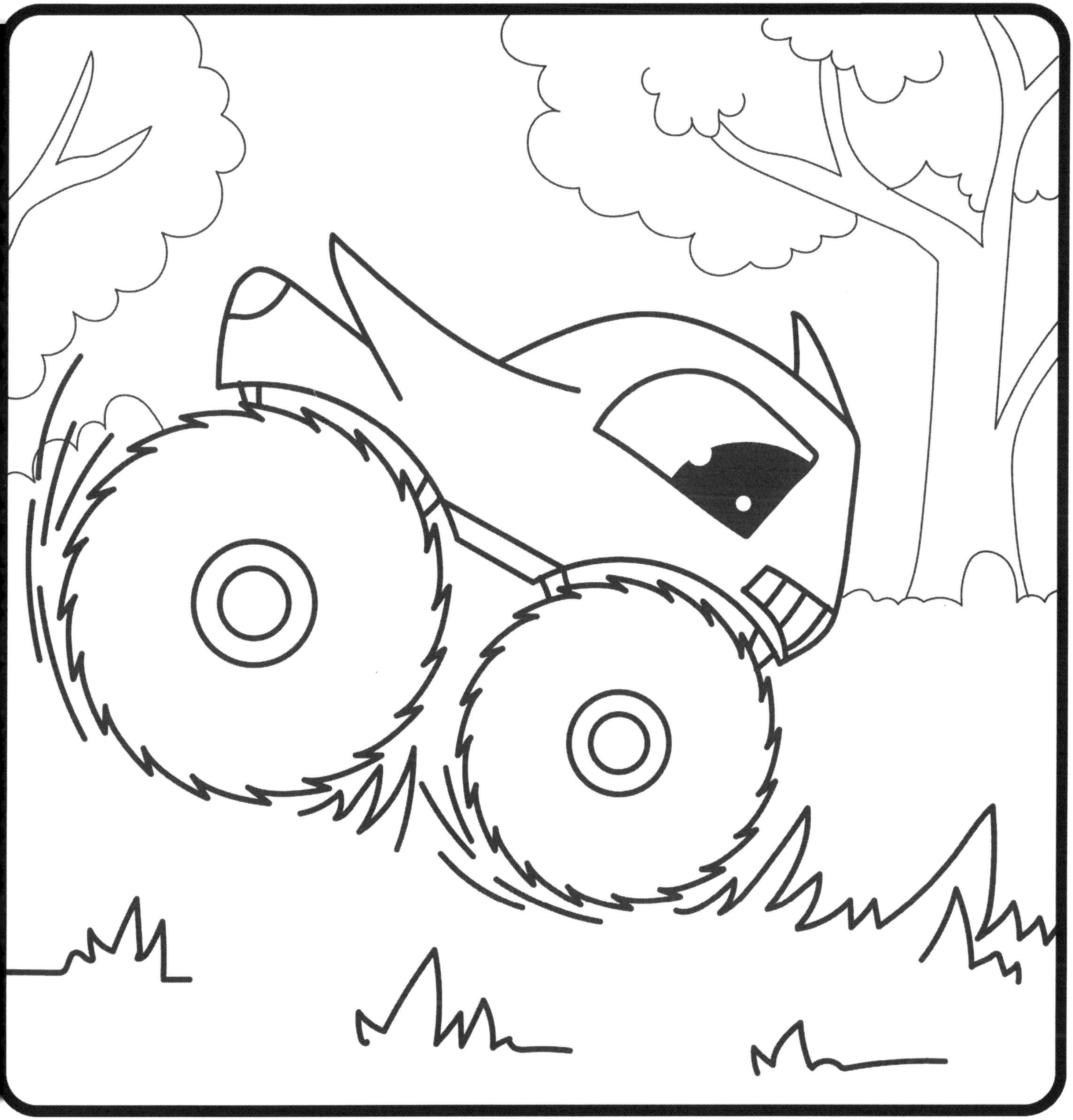

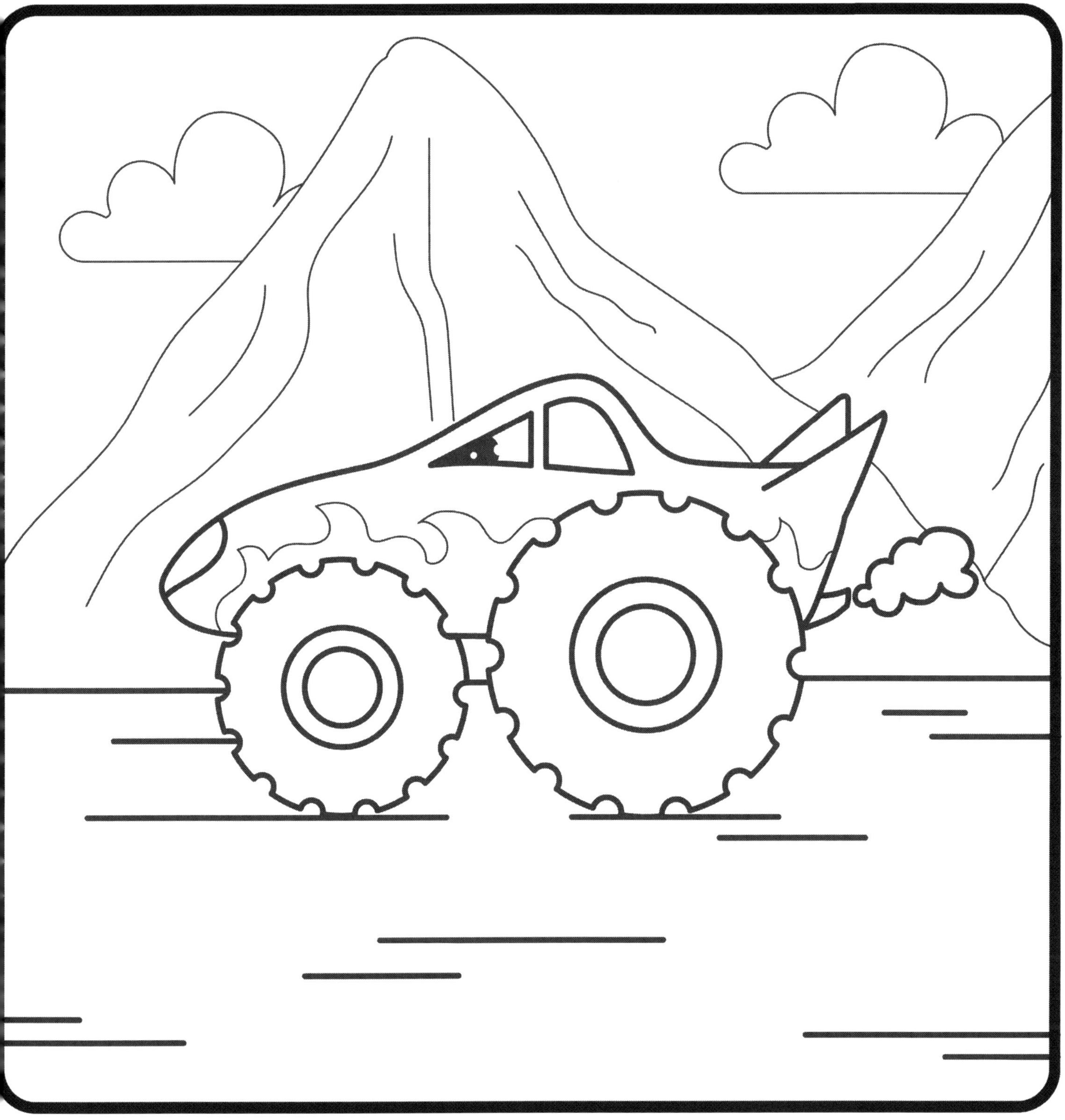

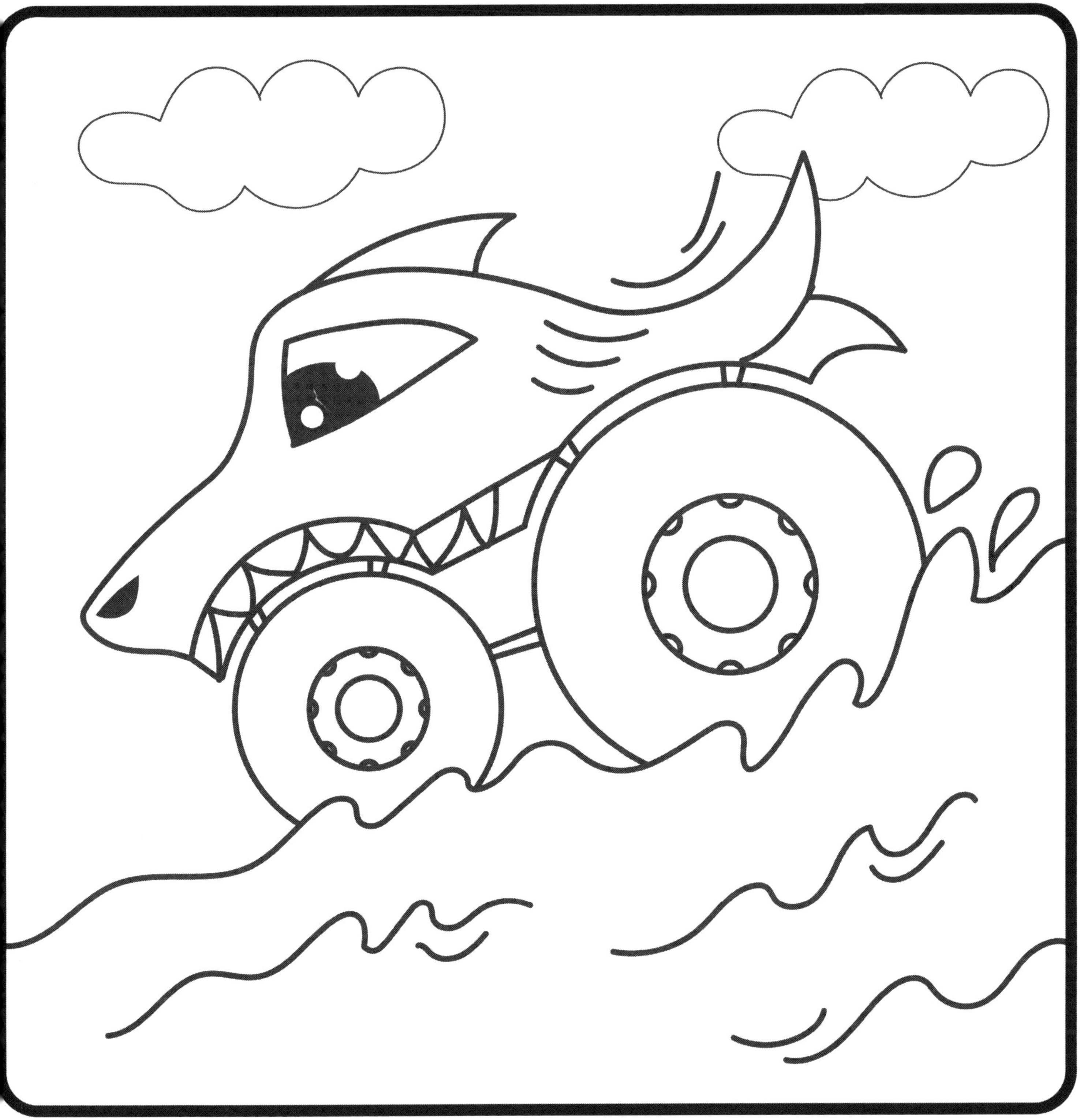

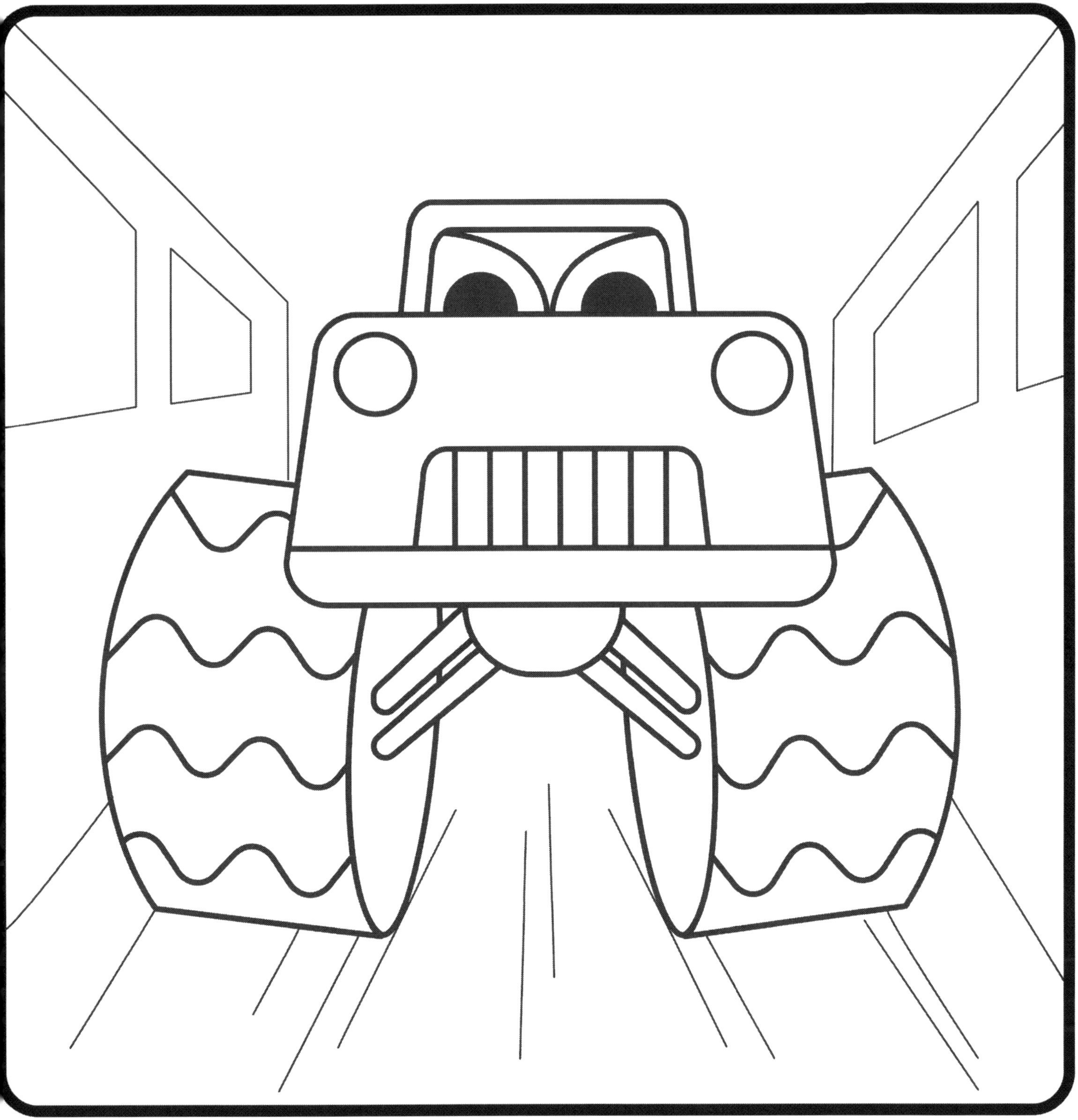

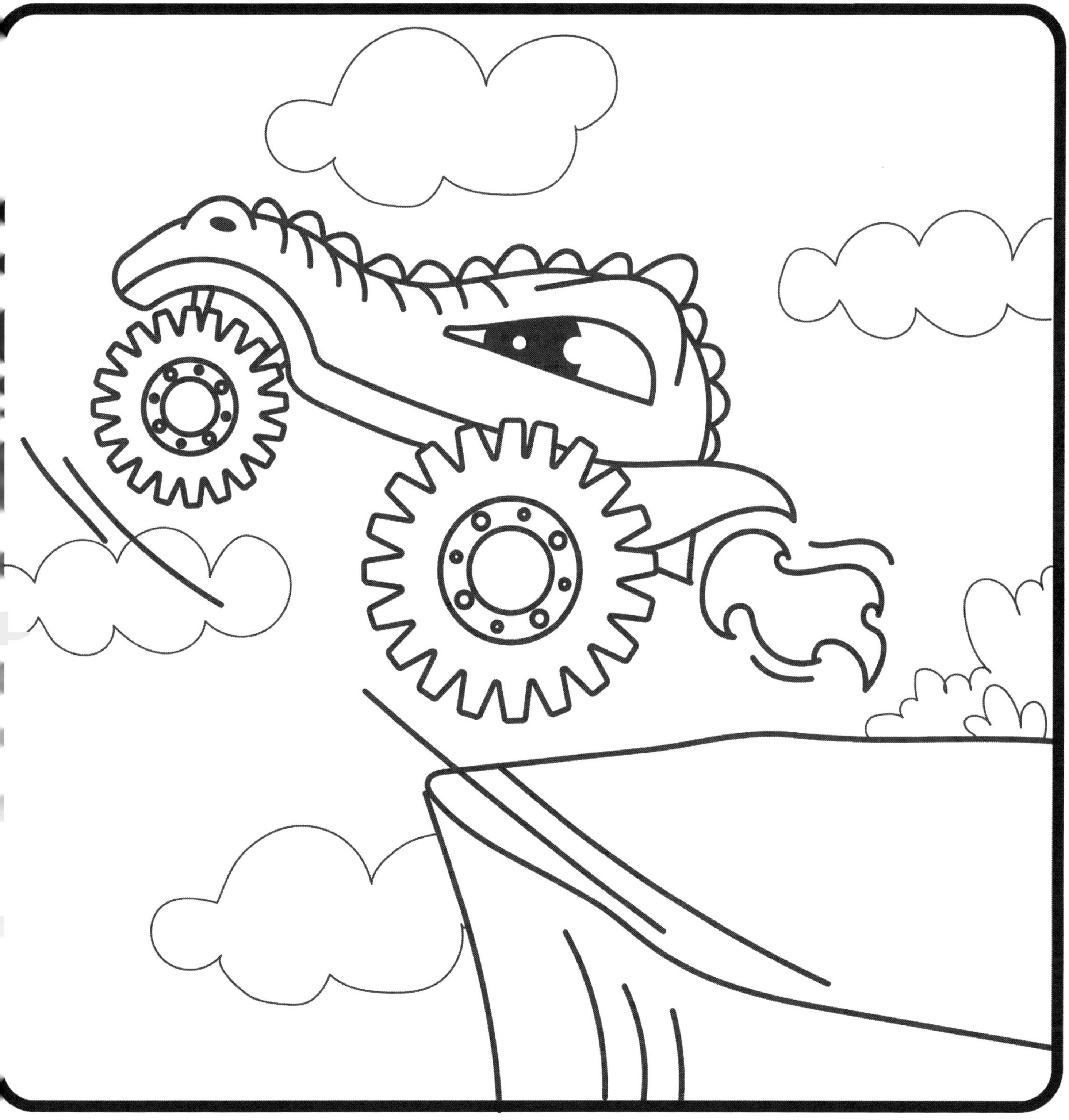

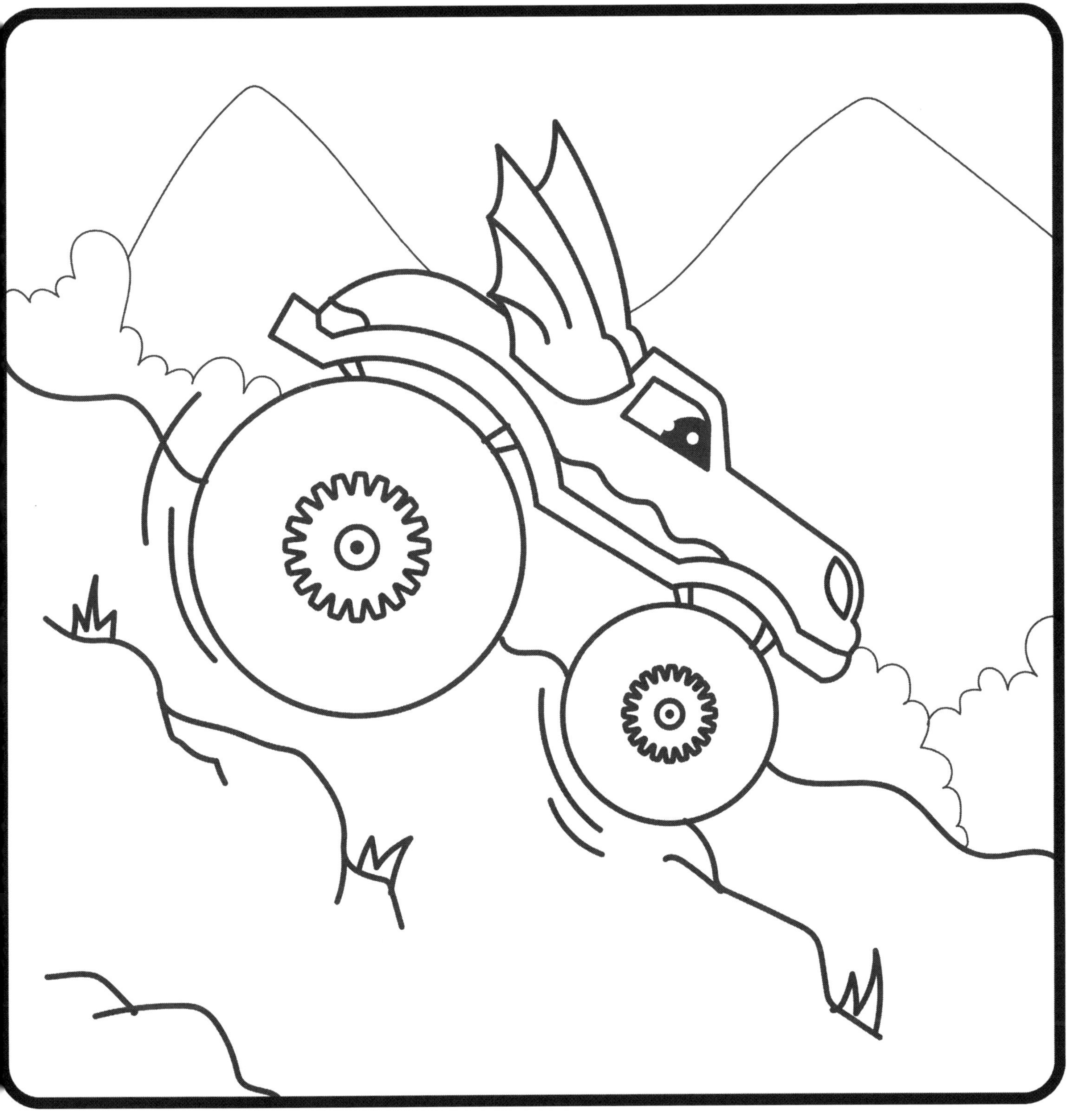

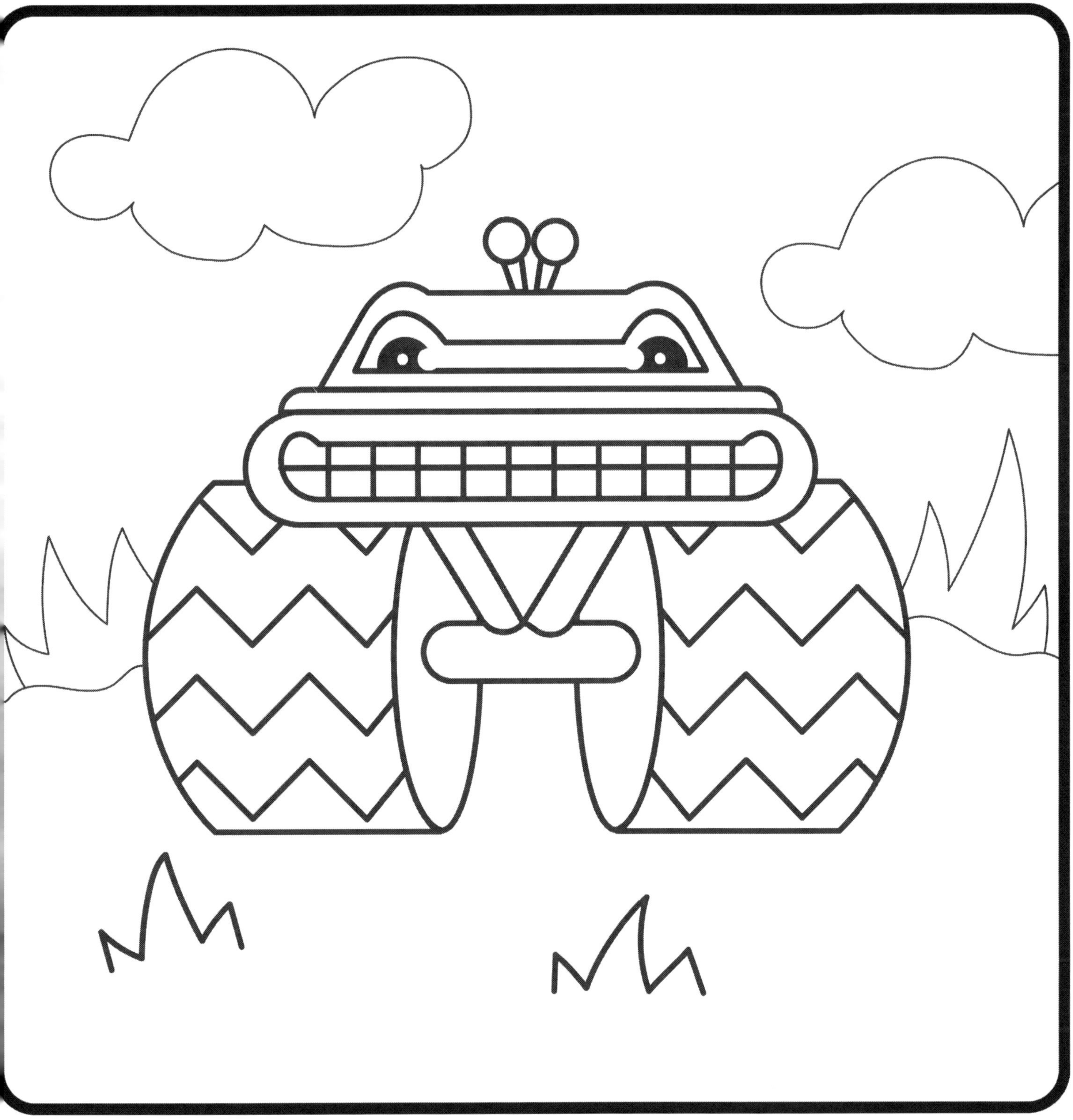

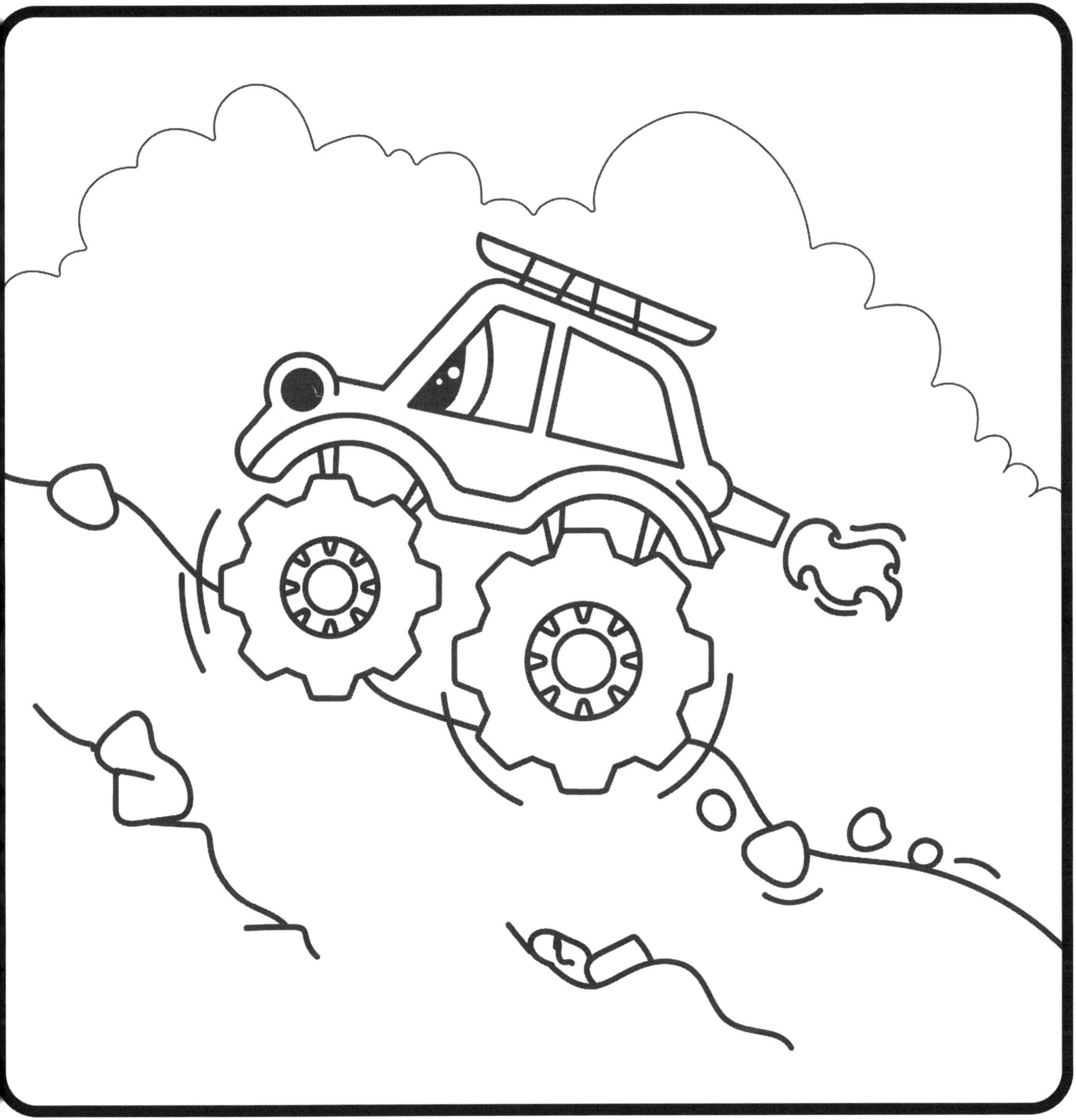

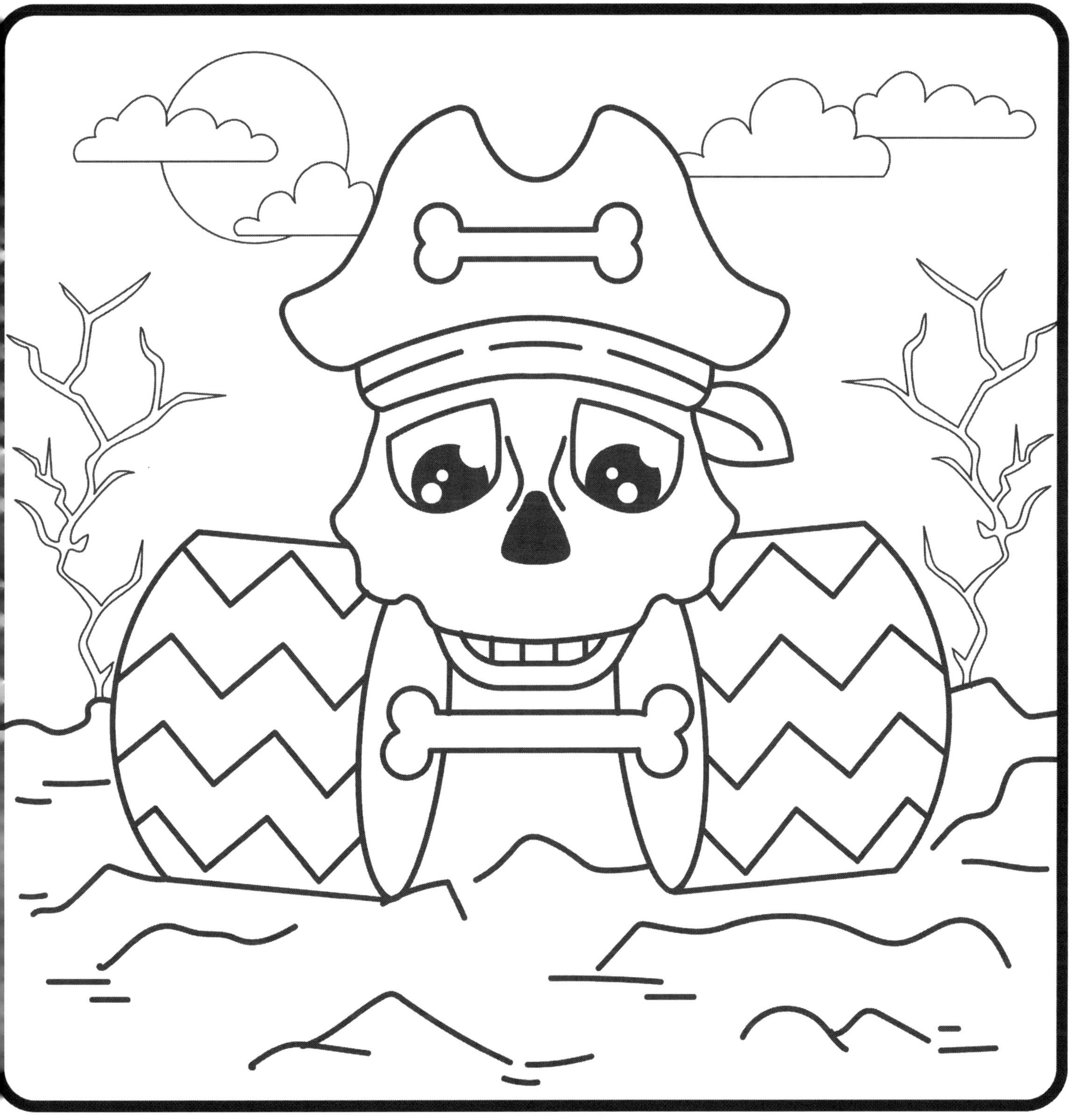

Made in United States
Orlando, FL
24 November 2024

54372119R00026